How to Increase Productivity in a Business

A Step by Step Guide to Business Productivity Improvement

I0462870

By Meir Liraz

Published by BizMove
www.bizmove.com

Table of Contents

MEIR LIRAZ

1. Introduction

The aim of this guide is to provide small business owners and managers with an overview of how company productivity can be improved. It covers what productivity is, how it is measured, and what a company can do to increase it.

Why should productivity growth be a national concern? It is because, if too low, the Nation can neither improve its standard of living at home nor compete successfully abroad. Productivity growth affects wage negotiations, inflation rates, business decisions, exchange rates, a host of other economic, political and social conditions, and, therefore, every small business owner and manager.

The factors affecting both National and individual firm productivity are many and diverse. Nationally, changes in employment, hours worked, the educational, age and sex composition of the work force, levels of capital investment and savings, government regulations, capacity utilization, inflation, among others, all can affect, favorably or unfavorably, productivity rates.

There are many productivity factors the firm can manage. How well does the firm utilize new knowledge; is it working at an economy-of-scale level; are the employees highly motivated and loyal or is there labor unrest and high worker turnover; is the resource (human and capital) allocation maximizing established goals; and finally, what is the overall quality of the company's management? And, if management sees productivity as a problem, is there a commitment to establish a company-wide Productivity Improvement Program?

2. Establishing A Productivity Improvement Program

Recent studies indicate that the quality of management is the key to increasing business productivity. It is up to the managers to identify productivity problems and develop an appropriate program to solve these problems. In the past several years, many of the Nation's most successful, larger corporations have started Productivity Improvement Programs (PIP). With profits slipping, their managements realized that improving productivity was the key to improving income; that only through an efficient and effective utilization of resources could they remain competitive and profitable.

The following Productivity Improvement Program outlines the key elements of programs successfully used by many companies including such giants as Honeywell, Westinghouse, GM and Ford.

Key elements of a Productivity Improvement Program (PIP):

1. Obtain Upper Management Support. Without top management support, experience shows a PIP likely will fail. The Chief Executive Officer should issue a clear, comprehensive policy statement. The statement should be communicated to everyone in the company. Top management also must be willing to allocate adequate resources to permit success.

2. Create New Organizational Components. A Steering Committee to oversee the PIP and Productivity Managers to implement it are essential. The Committee should be staffed by top departmental executives with the responsibilities of goal setting, guidance, advice, and general control. The Productivity Managers are responsible for the day-to-day activities of measurement and analysis. The responsibilities of all organizational components must be clear and well established.

3. Plan Systematically. Success doesn't just happen. Goals and objectives should be set, problems targeted and rank ordered, reporting and monitoring requirements developed, and feedback channels established.

4. Open Communications. Increasing productivity means changing the way things are done. Desired changes must be communicated. Communication should flow up and down the business organization. Through publications, meetings, and films, employees must be told what is going on and how they will benefit.

5. Involve Employees. This is a very broad element encompassing the quality of work life, worker motivation, training, worker attitudes, job enrichment, quality circles, incentive systems and much more. Studies show a characteristic of successful, growing businesses is that they develop a "corporate culture" where employees strongly identify with and are an important part of company life. This sense of belonging is not easy to engender. Through basic fairness, employee involvement, and equitable incentives, the corporate culture and productivity both can grow.

6. Measure and Analyze. This is the technical key to success for a PIP. Productivity must be defined, formulas and worksheets developed, sources of data identified, benchmark studies performed, and personnel assigned. Measuring productivity can be a highly complex task. The goal, however, is to keep it as simple as possible without distorting and depreciating the data. Measurement is so critical to success, a more detailed analysis is helpful.

3. Measuring Productivity

In an informal sense, productivity is getting more bang for the buck or doing the right things right. But these definitions do not help much when actual measurement is required. For that, a more mathematical approach is needed.

Productivity is a ratio, a comparison of what is produced and what is used to produce it. It compares outputs with inputs, that is, it divides outputs by inputs. Output is a physical entity - a car, a lightbulb, a typed page, or a processed pay voucher. For measurement, an output must be countable over time, a direct result of identifiable activities, and homogeneous (don't mix apples and oranges). Inputs can be classified into four types: labor, materials, capital and energy.

Each input can be used as the basis of a partial measure of productivity, depending upon circumstances. Labor productivity, for example, is measured by dividing output by hours worked, number of employees, or labor cost. Capital productivity is arrived at by dividing output by money invested or machine hours used. Materials productivity is output divided by units of materials used, units of scrap, or money spent. And energy productivity is output divided by units of energy consumed (like BTU's), or money spent.

Labor productivity (output = hours worked) is used by the government as the measure of the Nation's productivity. Many large, diversified companies, however, now use all four inputs to determine what is called Total Factor Productivity. In a purely office environment, since labor is the key input, some organizations use what is called the Administrative Productivity Index (API). It divides work output such as typing, loans serviced, clients interviewed or invoices processed by total hours worked to produce the administrative output. So the API essentially is a labor productivity measure.

Outputs and inputs can be measured in physical units or values or both. For example, an input unit for labor is hours and for value is dollars. A unit of output is the physical count of something and its value is its base selling price. If value (the dollar) is used as the basis of measurement, inflation must be accounted for to maintain a true value over time in constant dollars. Thus, all input and output values usually are tied to the Producer Price Index of each input and output (this compensates for the impact of inflation) to maintain valid input-output and value relationships in constant dollars over time. In other words, if revenues from product A increased 20% over last year, but its price increased by 8% to account for inflation, the real increase in dollar output was 12%. Yearly comparisons must be done using constant dollars. If the company mixes dollars and units, it still must deflate the dollars to maintain a valid relationship between physical quantities and value.

Another complicating aspect of measuring productivity is that not all inputs are equal and not all outputs are the same. Some production processes are more labor intensive than others; some use a variety of different labor skill (value) levels. Output products also change in quality and composition over time. So the process of weighing inputs and outputs to account for their relative values must be done before a truly accurate productivity measure is possible.

The point to remember is, whether employing a partial or total productivity measurement, whether for service or industrial application, or whether the business is large or small, all inputs and outputs must reflect constant values and true mixtures. To do this, all factors must be deflated and weighed.

One final technical consideration, productivity measurements should be indexed to facilitate comparison. Index each input and output measure to a base year and assign each measure the number 100. This makes it easier to calculate percentage changes over time.

Measuring productivity is time consuming and demanding: inputs and outputs must be defined, appropriate formulas developed, worksheets for keeping count printed, data collected, and calculations made. But the result will be more than just some numbers. Productivity measurement will provide a tool to assess the efficiency and effectiveness of the company, to forecast investment requirements, and to estimate the impact of cost increases or technological advances. The results do justify the effort required.

4. Industry Examples

So much for theory and mechanics. In practice, how have various businesses and industries actually gone about improving productivity? In the banking industry, for example, there has been revolution in productivity in the past decade. Through the use of computers, magnetic ink character recognition equipment, and mechanizing various repetitive operations, there has been a 50 percent reduction in labor requirements for check handling between.

Studies on the cosmetics industry show that through improved technology and by utilizing larger plants, it maintained a solid 4% annual manufacturing productivity increase. Economies-of-scale seem to have been the key factor here since plants with 500 or more employees were 37% more productive than the smaller ones. Studies on administrative productivity programs indicate that improved productivity comes from standardizing administrative procedures, streamlining operations, and increasing computer applications. These examples illustrate the importance to productivity of both advanced technology and proper management.

Different businesses use different measures of productivity. Airlines traditionally have used passengers boarded per employee and revenue ton-miles per employee as partial productivity measures. The Bell System has developed a sophisticated productivity program and integrated it into its overall budgeting and planning activities. The Bell program is worth a closer look.

Bell uses two Partial Productivity measures-volume of business per employee and number of phones served per employee. Both measure labor productivity. Bell also uses three Total Factor Productivity (TFP) measures to determine overall corporate performance.

One TFP measure emphasizes total output, the others gross and net value added.

Bell's TFP inputs are capital, labor, and materials. All are reported in current dollars, deflated, weighed, averaged, and indexed to arrive at a single Total Input Index. Hecause of the great variety of Bell products and services, output is measured in current revenues, not physical units. Again, the revenue dollars are deflated. All categories of revenues are then summed to arrive at a total dollar output figure. That total is indexed to arrive at a single Total Output Index. Finally, the output index number is divided by the input index number and the resulting figure is the Total Factor Productivity Index for the company. The percentage change over time in the TFP Index is Bell's key measure of the entire company's productivity.

Bell uses this TFP model to track productivity trends, to compare them with industry norms, and to plan long term. They also combine productivity with traditional financial analysis to determine the impact on net income of productivity growth, price change, and many other variables.

A wide-range of businesses, from small to the Bell System, have implemented successful productivity programs. Their experiences have shown that effective programs are thoroughly planned, technically correct, and fully communicated.

5. How to Increase Employee Productivity

It is conceivable for you to have more employees than the competition yet your company produces less and for you to have disgruntled, low-output employees even though you pay your employees more than the competition pays theirs. Productivity surveys and case studies indicate that increased worker motivation and satisfaction can increase worker output. Progressive, innovative managers now achieve productivity gains with human resource management techniques that go beyond pay incentives.

This Guide discusses how to increase worker output by motivating with quality of work life concepts and by tailoring benefits to meet the needs of employees. Cost: enlightened human resource management probably costs no more than employee turnover (hiring and training new employees), unwarranted pay increases, and low productivity. Benefit: better productivity; loyal, efficient workers; higher quality work, and increased likelihood of staying in business.

The essence of employee motivation and effectiveness is the manner in which they are managed. A direct relationship exists between effective management (i.e., providing a work environment that simultaneously achieves company goals and employees' goals) and modern human resource management.

Your management success is judged by your skill and knowledge in recognizing and assessing issues that concern employees and by your ability to resolve these concerns with employee help and satisfaction.

Do your employees know how you judge and measure their performance?

Do you provide and encourage individual development with training and educational programs?

Do you trust your employees and rely upon their knowledge?

Do you let employees make decisions?

Do you have timely, accurate, open two-way communication with your employees?

If you answer no to all of these questions, you probably are an unsatisfactory human resource manager and have (or will have) employee-productivity problems.

6. Quality of Work Life

Getting high quality job performance from your employees depends on giving employees opportunities for their personal growth, achievement, responsibility, recognition, and reward.

Pay - money - is the primary need and reward. Once the compensation (pay and benefits) is established properly, it is necessary to use other means to further motivate and improve your work force's output. The basis of all job enhancement efforts is your recognition of employees' desire to do good work, to assume responsibility, to achieve and to succeed.

Changes to consider in creating a new quality of work life atmosphere include:

From: detailed job descriptions with specific tasks and rigid instruction for how to do the work

To: Flexible, diverse work assignment allowing self-regulation, variety and challenge;

From: Structured chain of command, managers making decisions and supervisors bossing

To: Worker involvement in planning, decision making and operating procedure;

From: Hierarchical channels of communications;

To: Direct, fast two-way communication

From: Limited on-the-job instruction

To: Advanced training, educational and career development opportunities;

From: Job specialization in one task

To: Leeway allowed for every employee to complete many task by crossing lines of specialization;

From: Obscure, irregular job evaluations

To: Objective job performance standards with measures fairly administered;

From: Careless or neglected safety and health conditions;

To: Clean, safe and healthful working conditions.

The quality of work life technique is to involve your employees by sharing the management responsibility and authority with them - the workers who do the job.

7. Flexible Benefits

Compensation costs - salaries, wages, and benefits - are a large and increasing part of operating expenses; yet, productivity can decline among workers who get more pay and benefits. Workers are productive with fair pay tied to performance. Ironically, not all employee motivation and productivity problems are solved by pay raises and promotions. It isn't necessary to make pay adjustments beyond a fair industry-wide (market place) level.

The tailoring of benefits to satisfy specific needs is part of the quality of work life technique. It is a way to maximize the amount of labor costs going to the employee and to maximize your return on these costs without increasing across-the-board expenses. By making a special effort to satisfy individual employee needs, you reinforce the motivational value of the flexible benefit.

For example, you can reduce unwanted employee turnover and related recruiting, hiring, and training costs by shifting these costs from developing new employees to keeping experienced employees. You can motivate an employee to increase productivity by providing opportunities for career development (training or schooling).

At the same time you have improved the worker's skills and shown recognition of the worker's value and aspiration. A tailored benefit can be worth as much to an employee as a pay raise. Such a benefit is practical because (1) it probably costs no more than worker unrest and diminished productivity and (2) it is probably less costly than a comparable pay increase.

Age, education, job experience, job fulfillment, marital status, and family size are considerations that determine the utility and attractiveness of a benefit. Different benefits appeal to different people. Everyone's needs are different. A younger employee might be motivated by having use of a company car. An older person may want more status like a title or a professional association membership. The list of possible employees benefits and their applications is nearly unlimited. To get the maximum value, you've got to tailor the benefit to the job and your business requirements and financial capability.

Think how you could use:

pre-tax thrift-savings programs

recreational programs

discounts

scholarships

personal financial planning

loans

tuition refund

profit sharing

company car

personal expense account

parking privileges

legal assistance

extra vacation

child care

job titles

professional or trade association memberships

travel

A flexible benefit is two-fold. Not only does the benefit satisfy some employee's specific need but it also communicates your concern to meet these needs, creating the kind of work environment that contributes to increased employee productivity.

You must recognize the productivity problem and the needs of your employees so that you can tailor the benefit to meet the situation. Beyond pay and statutory benefits that provide the most value to your business.

Salary Compression

Ralph is an experienced employee. You think he is good but he is complaining that his salary is not enough. You're puzzled and angry because you gave him a raise and a cost of living increase a month ago and the salary is competitive. Ralph seems ungrateful and his output is down. After talking with Ralph, you learn that he feels he should be paid more than Ed, a new employee. You hired Ralph two years ago at $62,000, a year. He's now making $68,500. But Ed, was just hired at $56,000. Ralph thinks he should have more to show for his two years experience compared to Ed, who is younger with no experience.

You realize that starting salaries have gone up at a faster rate than regular pay increases. Attracting educated employees was competitive. Result: the difference in pay got smaller between experienced and less experienced employees. This is called salary compression.

Your experienced employees don't like it. They will react negatively, slowing down and looking for another job, another promotion, or another raise. In this situation you could recognize Ralph's experience, tenure and value with flexible benefits.

Using quality of work life techniques to motivate and to reward employees can result in productivity gains. The ultimate goal, of course, is to achieve the maximum result from the least effort, the greatest profit for the least cost, the largest output from the smallest input. To work toward this goal you've got to know how productive your company is. Thus, you must define and measure productivity for comparison from time to time.

8. Employee Productivity Measurement

Definitions of and ways to measure productivity vary. A basic way to express productivity is productivity equals output divided by input i.e., productivity is the ratio of output to input, or simply output over input. The quantity of output is measured in units produced, dollars of sales, or any term that suits your need. The quality of output is measured by workmanship, adherence to standard, and absence of complaints. Input is measured by labor costs, hours worked, and number of employees. To be useful, measures must be as simple and as consistent as possible.

A simple and understandable method of productivity measurement is to divide total sales (output in dollars) by total compensation costs (input). Increases and prices are accounted for automatically; however, you must adjust for inflation. To compare productivity measures in different years, pick a base year and give it an index of 100. Then figure your ratio of compensation to sales and with that number calculate the index and compare the fluctuation of the indexes.

Suppose as follows:

Year	xxx1	xxx2	xxx3
Total Sales	$500,000	$550,000	$610,000
Compensation	$247,500	$275,000	$302,500
Ratio	2.02	2	2.02
Index	100	99	100

Compute the index by multiplying the output ratio for the given year by 100 and dividing that result by the output ratio for the base year.

$$\text{xxx2 Index of Productivity} = \frac{100 \times 2}{2.02} = \frac{200}{2.02} = 99.00$$

The figures are hypothetical and are not adjusted for inflation, but they show that productivity declined in xxx2 compared to the base year xxx1 and that in xxx3 productivity returned (increased) to the level of xxx1.

But you had ten employees in xxx1 and xxx2 and eleven in xxx3. So you could also measure productivity output (sales) in terms of hours worked. Assume each employee worked a 40 hour week of 2,080 hours a year.

	xxx1	xxx2	xxx3
Total Sales	$500,000	$550,000	$610,000
Hours Worked	20,800	20,800	22,880
Ratio	24.04	26.44	26.66
Index	100	109.9	110.9

This index shows more sales to hours worked in xxx2 over xxx1 and the same again in xxx3 over both xxx1 and xxx2. Productivity increased. How valuable was the new employee?

Using output over input, you can measure any activity and employee. A typist's productivity can be measured in terms of numbers of pages typed, a salesperson by number of customer calls or amount of sales. When deciding how and what to measure, consider what a person does, how well, how much, and how often.

The indexes measure the productivity increases and decreases that indicate changes in your company's performance. You need these measures so that you

1) can set goals and priorities,

2) know where you stand,

3) are motivated by objective reasons - by numbers, not subjective feelings, and

4) have a common basis of communication with employees, bankers and consultants.

Chancing the Change

For many, if not most, companies adoption of quality of work life and flexible benefits management techniques can dramatically change how things are done. It is difficult and risky to make these changes; however, such changes may be not only necessary but also the difference between companies that are competitive and companies that aren't. Experience shows that with proper consultation, planning, training, and implementation the innovative human resource management concept is becoming the standard for effective management.